Vanessa

the rib

vanessa bryant

Contents

Acknowledgments

First, to my heavenly Father and the author of my life, I owe it all to you. Thank you for instilling the vision within me, for surrounding me with people that support and love me endlessly, and for the beautiful life you have given me. I am grateful for my countless blessings and for your continual provision over my life.

Next, to my husband, who provides endless support in all things I do. Thank you for encouraging me to pursue the vision and for believing in me from the beginning. I am so grateful to go through this life with such an amazing partner.

To my beautiful children, you have made me a mother and in the process you've helped me discover a better version of myself that I never knew to be possible. For that I am grateful. Thank you for helping me grow and giving me an even greater purpose in this life. I hope to serve as an example to both of you that with God, passion, and perseverance, you can accomplish anything you want.

The Rib

To my parents, thank you for always believing in me and my ability to accomplish my goals. Mom, you are the epitome of a woman with great character and strength. You have taught me so many things about what it means to be The Rib, one of which is to always remember, "You can do all things through Christ who gives you strength." Thank you for instilling me with these words; they have encouraged me when I lost my confidence and have propelled me through to the completion of my greatest achievements.

To the community of women in my life, I am forever grateful for each of you. Your stories of strength, love, triumph, resilience, and courage have inspired me. Your words of encouragement have empowered me. Thank you for your unwavering support.

And lastly, to Cassie and Sessen, two women I admire and am forever indebted to for their help in bringing this vision to life. Your encouragement and confidence in me has been essential throughout this process. I knew exactly to whom I was going for the first steps of the editing and publishing process. Thank you for agreeing to work with me, and for your time, sincerity, and dedication to this project.

Preface

Dear Readers,

I firmly believe that we're all created for
a purpose. Some of us, from very early on, have
great understanding of what that purpose is.
Others spend years hunting their purpose, to
uncover the power that makes you uniquely
you.

The journey to uncover and intentionally live
out that purpose can be a challenge. Societal
pressures overwhelm and cloud our vision,
causing us to second-guess and to question
whether our journey is in the right direction.

I've always had a passion for people. I have
a caring and helping spirit. I love deeply, and
I want to see the best in other people. It is
important to me that I be remembered as
an individual who uplifts, inspires, and
encourages others to be their best. I just knew
that purpose would be fulfilled in my career, in
what I chose to do, because it felt as though my
career defined me as a person.

The Rib

Well, on my journey to find my purpose, I have learned that while my career is a piece of my identity, it is not the whole story. And although I love being a Registered Nurse, I have also found fulfillment in my roles as a wife, mother, friend, and sister, and in the overall evolution of my womanhood. Being the best in these roles has not only helped me to really grasp what life is about, it has also helped me to mature and accomplish various career goals.

Part of the reason I chose to become a nurse was that I find the body to be particularly fascinating, and while on this journey, I was reminded about a very important group of bones in our bodies: the ribs.

Although critical, the ribs do not get nearly the attention they deserve for the work they do. They protect our most valuable organs, including the heart and lungs. They allow the lungs to expand, facilitating breathing, a vital function of life. They support and protect the entire body.

The ribs are so important that God used them to make women. In Genesis, it states:

"So the Lord God caused man to fall into a deep sleep; and while he was sleeping, he took one of the man's ribs and then closed up the place with flesh. Then the Lord God made a woman from the rib he had taken out of the man and brought her to the man. The man said, this is now bone of my bones and flesh of my flesh; she shall be called woman for she was taken out of man."

Throughout my journey in discovering my individual purpose, I have been reminded that as a woman I was created with immense intention; that my role as a woman in my family, community, and throughout the world, is supremely valuable. To be The Rib is one of the most important responsibilities one could have, and despite the variations ribs have in different species, they all serve the same basic purpose: to provide protection and support.

This book is about the personal obstacles I have had to overcome in my journey as

The Rib

The Rib. It's about how I have learned
the importance of self-love and self-
appreciation, so that I may continue to carry
out my purpose with joy and contentment.
This book is my diary-like entries to all of you,
my fellow mothers, wives, friends, sisters, and
career women. I hope you find it relatable,
spiritual, encouraging, and most of all,
inspiring, so that you may continue your
pursuits with a greater understanding of your
unique and profound significance in this
world.

Entry | ONE

Dear Life Purpose,

I know you exist, but at times I have difficulty finding you.

It is abundantly clear to me that every individual has purpose and yet, while I understand this, I am also aware it is not always easy for one to find that purpose.

We do not exist or journey through life merely as a result of evolution, happenstance, or coincidence. *We are beautiful creatures, amazing, divinely, and intentionally constructed.* These are the words I spoke to myself as I sat crying on my living-room floor, next to a box filled with everything from my desk at work. I felt like everything I had worked so hard for had been reduced to whatever was left in that cardboard box.

I was entering a new chapter of life: I would now be a stay-at-home mom. And while this decision was one I made because I thought it was best for my family, it was still difficult to accept. It wasn't until that moment, sitting on my floor, staring at that box, that it hit me: My life was shifting and moving in a direction I had not planned for. Everything I had once known, once strived to achieve, once believed was exactly what I should be doing to reach my professional goals, had shifted so suddenly and I was devastated and fearful. Devastated at the thought of never reaching my full professional potential, and fearful of this new territory I was embarking on.

Having grown up in a household with working parents and never having prepared for this as a possibility in my life, it felt so foreign. I questioned: *Would I be good at it? Would I enjoy it? Would my children appreciate it? And would my husband fully understand and appreciate the sacrifice I was making?*

This change in my life felt as though I had lost complete understanding of what I knew God's purpose was for me. On one hand, I felt blessed for my husband's job and his support that made it possible for me to stay home. On the other hand, I felt like I had no idea who I was anymore. My days were now spent at home with an infant and no adult interaction, dressed in frumpy workout clothes with my hair pulled back, and overwhelmed by the seemingly endless tasks that needed to be done around the house and the impossibility of fitting it all in between the naps, bottles, and diaper changes. The negative self-talk amplified, causing emotional instability and convincing me I had given up on my life's purpose. I began to feel myself sinking into depression.

While I was happy to sacrifice my personal plans to ensure our family's needs were met, I was scared of what that meant for my future. However, I also began to realize that while my priorities had shifted, I didn't have to make a choice between the two. As a matter of fact, I would be a better mother and wife if I continued to find ways to carry out my purpose and explore the ways in which my new role related to my purpose.

The Rib

You see, it was far from easy to come to this realization. It took praying through my tears, and speaking with friends that had been in similar positions, to realize that the fact that I wasn't working outside of the home, did not mean that I wasn't living out my purpose. For so long I believed career to be a synonym for purpose. I assumed that one carried out her purpose through her work and career, and never had considered that one may fulfill her purpose in other ways.

As I began to settle into my new normal, I challenged myself to see "purpose" in a different light. Yes, some people will use their unique gifts and skills to actualize their purpose in their career. However, this isn't the case for everyone. An individual's life purpose is not solely rooted in one's job; a seemingly obvious concept that, at the time, was new and especially profound to me. It was important for my well-being that I rediscover myself and feel purposeful again because, quite simply, part of my joy depended on it.

Dear Life Purpose

As women, we often feel that our individual identities have to be sacrificed for the roles we play in the lives of others. As I reached out to other women around me, I learned so many were yearning for the same thing I was: to feel valued, make a positive impact, and create the space in our lives for self-fulfilling activities while also excelling in our roles as wives and mothers.

I continued to pray for understanding and asked God to show me 1) how the things I was now doing related to my purpose, and 2) how I could find fulfillment in all that I was doing. I also made it a point to carve out time for myself and seek out things that allowed me to feel restored and rejuvenated enough to continue moving forward. It was during this process that I discovered the importance of self-care; I realized that when I make the time to nurture and care for myself, I am better equipped to navigate through my journey of carrying out my purpose.

Now, I feel confident in my role as The Rib. In my self-talk or conversations with others, when it feels like my purpose may be eluding me, I remind myself of Jeremiah 29:11: *"For I know the plans I have for you, declares the Lord, plans for welfare and not for evil, to give you hope and a future."* I look into the mirror and remind myself that while my circumstances may change, that does not shrink my value in this world. I have a purpose and I am always in control of how I use it.

Today, I resolve that I was created for a purpose.

Entry | TWO

Dear Funk,

You create a black hole in which I struggle to find any semblance of gravity or direction.

I sat on the couch, feeling as though I was sinking further into the cushions and deeper into the pit of my emotions. I looked around, overwhelmed by the sight of all the things that needed to be done. My eyes began to blink slower and slower, desiring to close and just go back to sleep. I asked myself, "Whom can I call to comfort me?" And just as quickly, I answered myself, "No one." And not because I believed no one cared, but because everyone has something going on. Why bother them with my silly troubles?

Then, instantly bringing me back to reality, I heard the sweet little voice of my daughter, "Mommy, mommy," she exclaimed. She's awake, I thought to myself, and I must muster up the energy to exude joy but inside I feel empty and I can't begin to imagine how I will regain the strength to pull myself out of this funk.

The funk is real. It is strong; and if given the power it will control you mentally and physically. Sometimes, we can pinpoint the exact situation that spawns this shift in our emotions, the reason for the funk we find ourselves in. Other times it's unexplainable. We wake up and are immediately consumed. You look around and everything feels a little off. You lack energy, happiness, drive, peace, and determination. And for some reason, you just feel defeated and deflated before the day even begins.

Regardless of our ability to identify the source of the funk, it's imperative that we understand that this is not our dwelling place and in those moments it's okay to pause, slow down, and put aside whatever may be necessary to create room to breathe. Give yourself the permission to step away from the long list of to-do's and to create a systematic approach to tackling the housework, children's activities, work deadlines, etc.

The busyness of everyday life can be overwhelming and challenging. The constant up and downs may lead to frustrations, and that is normal. However, many of us never allow ourselves the freedom to embrace the funk. We believe that if we just "keep going" and stuff those feelings away that eventually they'll disappear.

This is so far from the truth. When we consciously or subconsciously push these things aside, harbor them, and fail to take the necessary time to acknowledge and work through them, they become a breeding ground for negativity. It is in this space that we allow our internal dialogue to water the seeds of pessimism and disapproval; seeds that, like weeds, grow and take root in our lives.

In order for me to emerge out of the funk, I have to allow myself the time to acknowledge and assess what it is that has gotten me there.

The Rib

After doing so, I then ask myself what tools I need to overcome it. Is the source purely emotional? Do I perhaps need to find more time for meditation or self-reflection? Is it physical exhaustion? Do I need to focus on creating more balance within my schedule? Or is it quite possibly a combination of emotional and physical fatigue?

Most importantly, I have learned to accept that these feelings do not equate to failure and weakness. While these emotions are real, they do not have to be a defining moment and they won't last forever. I am able to persevere because I was created to do so. God does not intend for us to feel helpless. He desires for us to lean on him in these moments of gloom. I have spent many days repeating the words from an old hymn:

On Christ the solid rock I stand,
All other ground is sinking sand.
All other ground is sinking sand.
When darkness seems to hide His face,
I rest on His unchanging grace.
In every high and stormy gale,
My anchor holds within the veil.

I repeat this until I feel the negativity lift off of me, breaking me free of the weight I have been carrying. Then, in that same moment of relief, I stick my chin high and I reclaim my peace.

Today, I resolve to overcome negativity and regain my peace.

Entry | THREE

Dear Accountability,

At times, it's hard to live up to what you require, but I appreciate that you make me better.

It was early in the morning. The moon was still slightly visible, fading, preparing for the sun to make its way out. Typically, at this time I would still be in bed trying to squeeze in every last ounce of sleep I could, ensuring I was rested enough to take on the day's tasks.

However, this day was different. This day, I was up before the sun, bed made, coffee brewing, and a devotional in my hand. As I was sitting at the table, sipping my coffee and finishing the chapter in my devotional, my good friend called. I could tell by the tone of her voice that she was not expecting me to pick up the phone. She apologized, hoping she hadn't awakened me and expressing that she had just wanted to leave me a message before the day got going. But she knew me well enough to know that this morning was

The Rib

different: I was never awake at this hour.
She asked, "Is everything okay?" I told her that
I was trying something new, that I wanted to
start getting up before my daughter so I could
have some alone time and prepare my mind
and body for the day. She responded, "I love
this idea! I will help."

There is a saying that goes, "If you want to go
fast, go alone. If you want to go far, go
together." I know this saying well. Yet, I tend to
isolate myself because, quite frankly, it's
easier. Reaching out to others requires
a certain level of vulnerability that may
require overcoming an emotional struggle.

When I sat and pondered this quality about
myself, I realized that in some of the most
difficult times in my life, I was alone. And not
always in the physical sense, but certainly in
the emotional. I had to question why that was.
Was it my doing, the doing of others, or just
mere circumstance? I realized that in some
instances, though surrounded by people,
I chose to tackle my challenges alone because

Dear Accountability

I found that, at the time, the people around me did not have the best intentions for me. Conversely, there were times where people who I knew had my best interest at heart offered help, but I did not accept it because it required a vulnerability I was not ready to confront.

Motherhood has revealed to me the advantages in being vulnerable, so much so that I am now far more comfortable asking for help. By allowing myself to experience more vulnerability, the depths of some of my friendships have deepened and I have experienced more fulfilling and genuine relationships as a result.

Additionally, opening myself up to share my experiences with others has made me aware that these experiences were not unique to me, and many have dealt with similar struggles. As we opened up, sharing our truth and personal journey, no longer hiding behind fear, shame and judgment, I felt tremendous growth. And perhaps more importantly, the vulnerability created a space for us to grow together.

Something as small as my friend saying, "Hey, I hear what your goal is, and I will help," not only meant a lot to me, it propelled my success because I knew someone else cared and was invested. That level of accountability and the way it made me feel, inspired me to reach out to other friends and ask them how I could help hold them accountable in their lives.

Accountability, and allowing the space to be vulnerable, can be infectious. It enhances the satisfaction we feel within our lives and increases contentment. Now, I have learned to welcome moments of vulnerability, in which I can open up to those I trust about challenges I am facing and goals I am working toward in hopes of creating an environment of accountability that permeates all areas of my life.

It is even clearer to me that God's intent is for us to connect and lift each other up. It states in

Proverbs 11:14: *"Where there is no guidance, a people falls, but in an abundance of counselors there is safety."* Connection with others helps to negate loneliness and propels us to keep going. We need each other. This is how God designed us.

Today, I resolve to embrace vulnerability and foster an atmosphere of accountability.

Entry | FOUR

Dear Loneliness,

You have a way of making me question my relationships, while convincing me alone is the only option.

I sat on the plane thinking about the trip before me. I was on my way to visit a good friend I had not seen in a while. Although I looked forward to the time we would spend catching up—the inevitable fun and discussion of business ventures—I was worried that I would not be able to mask some of my emotional stress.

As I got my bags and saw her pull into the airport to pick me up, I was filled with excitement. I got into the car and we jumped right into conversation as though no time had passed between us. But not even 10 minutes into our conversation, my friend could sense I wasn't myself. It was evident for us in that moment that our original intentions for the trip needed to be shifted, and as good

friendships should allow, we adapted to
the need.

During the time we spent together, we were
rejuvenated through deep, open conversations,
while indulging in absolutely delicious meals
and peaceful massages. We allowed ourselves
to be present in the moment and I cannot tell
you enough how invigorating this experience
was for me. In fact, it was everything I was
yearning for, yet having a hard time
expressing. And without having to utter one
word, my friend knew exactly what I needed.

Through this experience I gained a more
personal understanding for Philippians 2:3-4:
"Do nothing out of selfish ambition or vain
conceit. Rather, in humility value others above
yourselves, not looking to your own interests
but each of you to the interests of the others."

When we fully invest in our friendships,
the power they have in our lives is
immeasurable. I used to think friendships

were measured by the number of friends that one had.

Thinking back to your earlier years, do you remember the popularity contests in junior high and high school? You know, back in the day when technology wasn't as advanced and not nearly as overused, and we would write notes to friends with pen and paper? I remember the feeling of complete joy to open my locker and find that I had received notes, folded into abstract shapes, in response to the ones I had written and slipped into friends' lockers.

And at the end of the year, there was nothing I wanted more than to be voted and remembered in the yearbook as someone everyone admired. I won Best Personality a few years in a row and was on top of the world because I thought that equated to popularity and meant that I had many friends.

However, as I grew older I came to quickly realize that you cannot quantify friendship.

The Rib

The friends you surround yourself with should be based on the quality and value they add to your life.

In various stages of my life, I began to develop my core group of friends. I started to find women who were relatable, encouraging, and admirable. Some of these women I value as mentors and as I continue to move forward on my journey, life brings along more incredible women for me to connect with. It has been life-changing. These women-friendships uplifted me from some deep, troublesome places.

And while my husband is my best friend and nothing can take away from that, the truth is that we, as women, need each other. We can relate to one another on a different level in times of joy and prosperity, and in times of defeat and frustration.

As I pondered the importance of my friendships, a small voice spoke to me asking, "What about your prayers?" Prayer is important in my personal guidance, and while

Dear Loneliness

I find it highly valuable and seek to always make time to pray and meditate, I believe God desires for us to connect to one another as well. He even has a way of using those around us to speak into our lives, as long as we are ready to listen.

Authentic friendships have a way of filling you up; and no, not in the way conversation over good food does. I'm talking about the emotional cup that must be filled in our lives. Friendship provides connection and reminds us that we are in fact, not alone. It is important that those connections coincide with our purpose. It is also important to understand that each friend is unique and does not serve the same purpose in our lives. As such, I've learned to value each friend for the unique way in which they are a part of my journey.

Additionally, do not neglect the impact you have on your friends and the ways in which that impact likely relates back to your purpose. Friendships should be give-and-take, requiring work and effort. So, let us be intentional in our friendships by ensuring we are equally contributing to the relationship.

While I may not always have the time or opportunity to go visit a friend as I was so fortunate to do in the story above, I have committed myself to make more of an honest effort to check in with my close circle of friends. It is important to me that I constantly contribute to creating a space where we all feel safe and comfortable expressing our emotions and unpacking our challenges with one another; ensuring that we move beyond surface-level relationships; and allowing ourselves to go deeper in conversation, letting all walls down and to be encouraging voices for one another. This has helped to diminish those lonely feelings and to remind me I am loved.

Today, I resolve to be cognizant of loving friendships that surround me and realize I am never alone.

Entry | FIVE

Dear Exhaustion,

You rob me of my strength and ability to pursue much of anything.

"You can't touch a woman who can wear pain like the grandest of diamonds around her neck."

–Alfa

As the blood ran down my hand and I could see the deep ruby tissue exposed at the tip of my thumb, I knew I needed stitches. Inside I felt frantic, realizing I needed help. Outwardly, however, I tried to keep a brave face for the two toddlers I was responsible for that day. The parent of the other child in my care was out of cell-phone reach and I didn't have two car seats to load the kids up for a trip to the emergency room. I had to find another solution until I was able to get help.

I pulled out my dusty first-aid kit and a tube of super glue. My daughter and her friend looked at me with deep concern as I did my best to

reassure them I would be all right, though
I wasn't fully certain I would be. I secured my
finger with super glue and Band-Aids,
replacing the Band-Aids every hour for
the next few hours until the bleeding slowed
down.

What started off with what I thought was
a great plan to keep the kids entertained
through the winter storm, turned into
a disaster. Later that evening when I was
finally able to get to the ER, the
physician looked at me with concern and said,
"If I may ask, why did you try and care for this
at home?" I answered, "It was my only option
until I could come in," going on to explain to
him what happened. He responded, "Well
kinda smart." To which I replied,
"Kinda stupid." I walked out of the ER with
eight stitches, feeling completely exhausted by
the day's turn of events.

During the ride home, while thinking about
everything that had taken place that day,
I realized that life is sometimes like this: it cuts

deep, unexpectedly. Life cuts when you're already exhausted, when you're trying your hardest, when you're near a breaking point. Yet, time and time again we find the inner strength to secure our wounds and keep fighting.

The situation also made me further analyze the strength of a woman and the load we bear in our workplaces, at home, and in our relationships. We women generally absorb the pain, the workload, and the emotions of others in hopes of helping those around us continue onward. This incident caused me to question why we do this.

Is it part of our nature? Have we been conditioned to do so? Are we doing this in fulfillment of expectations put upon us?

I am willing to bet that there have been many times that you were unaware of the trials, challenges, or difficulties faced by the strong women in your life, including your mother, friend, mentor, etc. Women have learned to manage their challenges in a way where we remain calm and suppress our inner angst. We have learned to "wear our pain like diamonds" and while it is not always easy, we make it possible.

Understanding all that is demanded in my role as a woman, I began to ponder why I typically haven't acknowledged these abilities as a superpower. Instead, I look in the mirror, discrediting the strength required to fulfill my roles every day. I don't take the moment to lift myself up, to speak back to my reflection with words of love and positive affirmations; I just continue to push myself harder and find ways to take on what comes along and get it done to the best of my ability.

However, we as The Rib need to realize the danger in not acknowledging our burdens, and continuing to put everyone before ourselves. As solid bones, ribs still have pliability at their base to allow for breathing, flexibility, and adaptation. We need to create the space and time to acknowledge our powerful abilities. We need to give ourselves permission to do the things that build us up so that we can continue to move in a positive direction.

It helps me to remember that I am "clothed in strength" (Proverbs 31) and that while life's chaos may be "cutting" into me, I can and will get through it; I always do. It may require a little bit of super glue to temporarily hold me together, but I will not allow life's struggles and exhaustion to make me feel defeated. We are capable of overcoming anything, and with our unique strength we have the ability to conquer anything we set our minds to.

Today, I resolve that I am clothed in strength and will not be defeated.

Entry | SIX

Dear Busybody,

You persuade me to continue at a pace that's hard to maintain and convince me to take on more than I can possibly handle.

Before the day began and patients flooded the waiting room, I took a moment to write an inspiring message on the board that hung in the middle of the nurses' station. On this particular day, in bold letters I wrote, **"Busyness does not always equate to productiveness."** Stopping what I was doing to prepare for the day ahead, I studied the quote and realized that I was in fact guilty of filling my time and not always feeling very productive.

As a nursing team, we sat together and strategized how we would aim to be intentional about everything that day, finding areas where we could increase our efficiency. At the end of the work shift, most of us felt that by being more mindful of efficiency at

the beginning of the day, we did accomplish
our goal of increasing productivity.

On my drive home from work, I contemplated
how I could be more productive in my
personal life as well. To this day, this often
replays in my mind, especially on the busy
days that come with motherhood.

In my role as a mother, I often feel like
a hamster on a wheel—moving fast but going
nowhere. There are always things to clean,
errands to run, play dates to get to, and on and
on and on. And once the day is over, it seems
as though the RESET button is pressed and
I prepare to start all over again the next
morning.

When I made the transition to staying at home
I realized that I had replaced the
accomplishable checklist of to-do's I had at
work with what now felt like overwhelming
responsibility that I could never seem to
conclude. In fact, friends began to greet me by
saying, "Hey, I know you have been busy..." or

Dear Busybody

"I haven't seen or heard from you in a while."
And while this was true—I had been busy—
I realized that I was staying busy with
an overbooked schedule that left me feeling
drained, exhausted, and extremely frustrated.
I was missing out on the things I wanted to do,
while still failing to achieve that sense of
accomplishment. I would often stop and say to
myself, "You have been busy, but what did you
actually accomplish today?"

One day, I read a daily devotional by
Lysa TerKeurst: "The woman who lives with
an overwhelmed schedule will often ache with
the sadness of an underwhelmed soul."
I realized that in all my busyness I needed to
be sure that I was both feeling accomplished
and fueling my soul.

The feeling of accomplishment gives me
restored energy to keep pushing toward
the next task or goal. I began to apply Lysa's
words to my life and made more time to
prioritize, minimize, and disconnect.

Now, I practice a self-check ritual asking myself the following:

1. Am I prioritizing my time by importance and necessity?
2. Am I minimizing my commitments to create more space for restoration?
3. Am I disconnecting from technology and social-media outlets and filling that time with meditation and self-care?

Today, I resolve to prioritize, minimize, and disconnect to improve my productivity.

Entry | SEVEN

Dear Popularity,

You speak loudly, warning me not to miss out and persuading me to always keep a full circle of friends. I am left feeling surrounded, yet lonely because many of these relationships are not authentic.

As we sat across from each other, sharing food and talking about friendships, my friend looked at me with concern and said, "Vanessa, make sure that everyone you have around you or in your corner deserves to be there." Her words immediately gave me pause. I began to reflect on my circle and whom I've opened myself up to. I had never really considered the question, "Do they *deserve* to be there?"

I consider myself an ambivert, meaning I know how to play the part in social situations but can also keep to myself and truly value alone time. Throughout life, I've fostered relationships with a core group of people I affectionately refer to as "my people"; the people I feel closest to. Yet as I shared with

The Rib

my friend some situations I was going through
with a few of these people, her words really
encouraged me to re-evaluate who it is
I consider to be "my people."

In this time of increased use of social media,
we may feel the need to acquire lots of friends
and to be part of many social circles. We may
feel the need to be involved in as much as we
can, to attend as much as we can, and to do for
others as much as we can. And while this is all
potentially very positive and helpful for our
growth and pursuit of our various goals, it
can also be extremely draining. I've realized
that the need to be involved in everything and
present for everyone has often emptied my
emotional cup, leaving me unhappy and feeling
dissatisfied. I constantly pour into others
without recognizing when my own cup needs
refilling. And doing so has also made it difficult
to distinguish friends from acquaintances,
friends from authentic connections, and
friends from "frenemies."

I also used to worry about the things I would miss out on, or the friend that may accuse me of not being there for them, or the missed networking party at my job or invitation to join a club. I conditioned myself to feel bad about saying no, or about removing myself from the relationship altogether.

Consequently, I ran myself ragged trying to be what people wanted me to be. I was worn out, and pretty soon I realized, while I had people around me, I felt alone. Something had to change.

I sensed the shift in the person and friend I became when I was confident that the people in my life were in alignment with my purpose. The people I surrounded myself with lifted my spirits and poured back into me, refilling my emotional cup. It is important we realize that the relationships we are involved in have a profound impact on our life. John Maxwell, in his book, *The 21 Irrefutable Laws of Leadership*, points out, "A leader's potential is determined by those closest to him." He goes on to refer to this principle as "The Law of the Inner Circle."

Now, I check in with myself regularly and ask if my relationships are meeting an emotional, physical, and psychosocial need. Are they bringing positivity and important influence? Or are they slowly robbing me of energy, satisfaction, and joy? How is my inner circle currently influencing my goals and my potential? Am I trying to pour from an empty cup? If so, I have learned to pause and evaluate why.

Through this new practice, I have given myself permission to disconnect from people and things that are not aligned with my purpose, understanding that sometimes people and associations are temporary and only intended for a season in our lives. Disconnecting from those that consistently drain rather than restore creates space for the people and things that fill me. In other instances, allowing pause has been a remedy for re-energizing relationships that may need a fresh start.

Additionally, I choose what I participate in wisely. Deciding where I spend my time and energy should be deliberate and not out of mere obligation and for the approval of others.

Today, I resolve to choose wisely whom I devote my time to, and to always seek genuine friendships.

Entry | EIGHT

Dear Insecurities,

You convince me that my physical appearance is never good enough and that my flaws diminish my ability to be loved.

As I held a picture of my pre-babies self and compared it to the person in the mirror, I began to weep. As I looked in the mirror, it was hard to find anything that seemed familiar. I remembered that even in my youth I was critical of my appearance and now, as an adult wishing I could go back, I felt sad for the girl who believed she had never been good enough. I realized I had never fully accepted myself, always focusing on my flaws and never spending enough time appreciating anything else. It was in this moment that I decided my mindset had to shift. I would embark on a journey to learn to love myself.

As I vulnerably expressed these emotions to some of my closest friends, we all found that we struggled with similar issues of self-acceptance. Among many women, the pressures to be of a certain size and to look a certain way are all too common. I began to wonder if we as women were potentially allowing body image and the ways we feel about our bodies impact other areas in our lives. Are we allowing our insecurities about our physical appearance to spill into our subconscious thoughts, creating insecurities in all that we do?

I've always admired women who have found acceptance in who they are, who look at their reflection with assurance and love. As a result, they exude confidence, and our ability to do this says a lot about who we are.

However, it's one of the most difficult things to do, to look in the mirror and simply admire everything about who you are. There is power in being proud of the person you are, despite your imperfections. Honoring yourself—flaws and all—teaches you not to be reduced to the expectations of others, nor limited by societal norms. Self-love teaches us how to stand on our own, to be comfortable in our skin, and to write our own rules. When we live unrestricted by the opinions of others—real or imagined—we unlock our highest potential.

In my journey to find the power of self-love, I found restored confidence and increased contentment. This restored confidence gave me the power to believe that I could live out my purpose and achieve goals I had set for myself. I realized criticizing myself and feeding myself lies of not being good enough, robbed me of my confidence and fostered insecurities. Over time, the steady stream of negativity and insecurity saturated my mind, and I developed limiting and self-sabotaging behaviors that drew me further and further away from reaching my potential. Yet, as I began the practice of intentionally releasing the negative thoughts, doubt slowly grew into self-assurance.

When I stopped comparing myself to others or even to my old self, I felt increased contentment. I began to accept where I was in

the moment, trying not to focus on the things
I couldn't change. I also began making realistic
goals to achieve the things I desired for myself.
I learned to appreciate the journey and
I can now say with confidence, my body is
a beautiful expression of my individuality. Self-
assurance has eliminated self-doubt, allowing
me to freely and fully celebrate my
accomplishments without hesitation.

Now, when I look in the mirror I see strength,
love, and perseverance. I speak words of
positivity to my reflection and whisper to
myself, *"I am fearfully and wonderfully made"*
(Psalms 139:14). I no longer rely on the love
and affirmation of others to fill me up. Instead,
I first seek and attain fulfillment from within.
I don't focus on the flaws and the things I am
not.

Dear Insecurities

I focus on what I am and the possibility of what
I can be. I recognize my imperfections to be
a part of my story, the body of art that is me.

**Today, I resolve to love myself in spite of
my flaws.**

Entry | NINE

Dear Self-Doubt,

You stand in the way of my ability to be a visionary, to follow my dreams and share my gifts with the world.

We packed the car full, leaving barely any room to see out of the rear-view mirror. It was our first road trip as a family, with our baby girl. While the moon was still high, the stars still shimmering and baby still sound asleep in the back seat, my husband and I took advantage of the quiet time to catch up with one another, something that the hustle and bustle of our days had kept us from.

We unpacked our future goals and talked about how far we had come. Nervous, because I was unsure of how it would be received, I decided to open up to him about something I had had on my mind; I wanted to write a book. He paused. I could see he was processing everything I had said, but nonetheless, his pause made me uneasy. *Would he approve? Does he think I am crazy?*

After his brief contemplation, he began to give me ideas and suggestions of titles and how to make it the most successful. He thought it was a great idea and I could feel his support through his genuine enthusiasm. I recognized in that moment that any question I may have had regarding whether or not he would support me in this venture, had nothing to do with him and everything to do with my own self-doubt.

Self-doubt can keep us from following through with a life-changing vision, hold us back from accomplishing a goal, and prevent us from taking very important steps forward in our life. Each time I sat down to write more of this book, I felt the doubt rushing over me, so strongly sometimes that I would find something else to do. I told myself this project would never be a success and convinced myself to quit countless times.

However, my desire to positively impact the lives of others always motivated me to start again. As time went on, I decided to take the doubt I was feeling and redirect that energy into positivity and exploration.

I began by asking myself the following questions: *Is there a specific source of this doubt? Am I doubting myself because I have skipped some steps along the way? Do I have the right intentions? Do I need to better prepare myself or complete more research? Do I need an accountability partner or mentor? Or, is this self-doubt rooted in fear and nothing more than my own insecurities? Do I need to build my self-confidence, improve my positive self-talk, and learn to appreciate the small steps along the journey?*

Not only did I start to redirect my thoughts, I started to connect how the ways I felt about myself might impact my daughter. If the roles were reversed, I would never want her to doubt her abilities. I'd want her to know that she is full of potential and can achieve anything she desires with dedication and hard work. I would never want self-doubt to keep her from trying. Additionally, I'd want the source of her confidence to come from within and not from the applause and approval of others. I would encourage her to move past her fears, failures, and missteps, and to understand that to dwell on these feelings would only leave her feeling defeated.

Imagining the things I'd want my daughter to know created a different type of personal accountability. I wanted to not only teach her these lessons but to demonstrate them. One day, I'd want my daughter to say, with her head held high and chin lifted, that she learned to be self-assured, confident, and courageous because these were the qualities she had witnessed in her mother.

There is a saying that goes, "Self-doubt kills more dreams than failure ever will." When we free ourselves of self-doubt, it creates space for us to reach our full potential. We are no longer bound by self-limiting mindsets and behaviors, unlocking our ability to be more creative, more successful, and ultimately happier in our lives.

Today, I resolve to believe in myself and my ability to do anything.

Entry | TEN

Dear Patience,

You truly are a virtue and every day the amount of you I possess fluctuates. I truly appreciate your life lessons.

I remember the exhaustion I felt while a student in nursing school, working hours upon hours on projects and reading textbooks with what felt like, at the time, no end in sight. I recall waking up for early-morning clinicals, exhausted and looking for the motivation to get out of bed. I took deep breaths in and out, all the while reminding myself to have patience, for all of my hard work would soon pay off.

Fast-forward to the present and now, in my role as a mother, I find that I give myself the very same advice: inhale and exhale patience daily. Motherhood is ever-evolving, there is no finish line, and as a mother your job is never complete.

The Rib

Patience has been one of the most important lessons I've learned in my life and although there have been many experiences that have taught me this lesson, there has been no greater teacher than motherhood. From the moment I found out I was pregnant, through the challenges of pregnancy, and then having to raise my child, the entire journey of motherhood has been a lesson in patience.

One day, as I hurried around the house preparing my daughter and myself to tackle the long list of to-do's, my daughter suddenly exclaimed, "Mommy! Mommy!" With concern in her eyes, she looked at me. Not noticing anything obvious, I wondered what the problem was. She then said, "I'll be patient, I'll be calm, right?"

In that very moment all I could do was smile because my daughter was reminding me of my own teaching. For weeks I had been focusing on this affirmation with her, because I wanted her to understand that sometimes the pace with which we desire things to happen is not the same pace with which we can go. And at only two years old, she could sense that in this moment, my energy was low and the pace I was going was too fast. I needed to decelerate. I responded, "Right! I'll be patient, I'll be calm." Immediately, I felt a shift in my energy, releasing unnecessary pressure and allowing myself to slow down and regain control.

We must learn to slow down. Being intentional about the moment isn't easy but when we are constantly focused on what lies ahead, we can never truly appreciate where we are nor where we have been.

With regard to motherhood, I tend to seek advice from other moms about the next phase or stage. I wanted to be at least partially prepared for what was to come. With my daughter, I was always eager, sometimes even anxious, for what was coming next. After having my second child—my son—I realize now that the moments I eagerly anticipated with my daughter always came faster than expected, and soon I began to yearn for days past. With new milestones came new challenges and my daughter's increased desire to exercise greater independence (which was also hard to accept).

Now, with my son, I try to live in the moment. I enjoy each stage, realizing that it will all pass so quickly. Discovering the ability to live in the moment has given me newfound appreciation and peace as a mother.

When we practice patience it creates room for understanding of others and ourselves. It improves our decision-making and supports our ability to act rationally. Overall, patience helps us to be better spouses, friends, co-workers, parents, and business owners. Demonstrating patience may require you to trust God a little deeper, and to declare, *not my will but whatever your will Lord, may it be done in your perfect timing because I have faith that good things come to those who wait.*

Dear Patience

Patience is not easy, but it is necessary. In a world increasingly obsessed with speed and convenience, it's important to recognize that we have the ability to regulate the tempo of our lives.

Today, I resolve to accept the pace of my journey and to demonstrate patience through the process.

Entry | ELEVEN

Dear Gratitude,

You are powerful, and without you as a constant in my life, happiness is difficult to find.

As we sat in homes built from remnants of what was left behind from the recent hurricanes, we listened to people tell stories of how their belongings were washed away as the water filled their homes and how they held on to one another, fighting to survive and praying for the storm to pass. For some, this was not the first time they had experienced such devastation.

It was 2012 and my husband and I were in the beautiful country of the Philippines. We went with a Christian-based organization to help various communities throughout the country that had been affected by Tropical Storm Sendong. We were in awe of the people and the genuine happiness they exuded, especially in light of all the devastation surrounding them. They thanked God for

the things that remained and showed extreme
gratitude for our presence. And their gratitude
was authentic: Their smiles radiated from
the inside out and there was a sense of sincere
happiness, despite their circumstances. We
thought that we were going to the Philippines
to encourage and lend a helping hand but
instead, they helped us put things into
perspective.

With smiles, they taught us that gratefulness is
not to be expressed in exchange for fulfilled
expectations, great finances, or the acquisition
of possessions. Rather, it is something that we
can choose to exercise regardless of our
current station in life. I am still convinced this
experience fed more into our lives than we did
for those that we sought to help.

As a Millennial, I feel it's becoming increasingly
difficult for my generation to find
the satisfaction and genuine gratitude so
evident in the Filipino people we met.
Advancements in technology and social
media have made it even more challenging not

to fall into the trap of constantly comparing our lives to others'; it also does little to quell our desire to always want more. It's hard to be content with where we are and what we have because we are constantly being told that not only is the next best thing coming but also, that we need it. I find myself asking, "How do I stay grounded in my happiness? How do I remove the stipulations placed on my happiness and just simply choose to be happy?"

I recognize how easy it is for me to get swallowed up in the "never satisfied" mindset, leaving me feeling disheartened and unenthusiastic about life. Admittedly, there have been moments in my life where I was guilty of being a Negative Nancy: the one so overwhelmed with frustration, she has difficulty finding the positivity in life. This negative energy has only left me feeling empty.

Life is a challenge. It is not always easy and sometimes, you are swimming against strong currents. However, my trip to the Philippines taught me that the most joyful people in

the world have learned to see past difficulties
by choosing to focus on the beauty in
the simplicity of everyday life.

Thinking about my time in the Philippines,
I recall being particularly struck by one man.
One day, as we were walking through
the market in the city of Cagayan de Oro, music
began to play from an old stereo. The music
was familiar—it was a popular song from
a well-known American rap artist, and
the song had been made even more popular
because of the dance that accompanied it.
The kids in the market started to fill the street,
dancing in sync. I knew the dance as well and
I joined in.

As I was dancing, a man came up to me.
Though missing some teeth, his smile was big
and infectious. His clothes were dirty and
tattered and he had no shoes. But he danced.
He danced, smiling wide and exuding pure joy.
This man, despite his circumstances, was able
to find the joy in the moment. He didn't allow
his bare feet to keep him from dancing with

sheer happiness. And I realized in that moment that if this man could find a reason to smile, we all should be able to find something to smile about and be grateful for.

Gratitude is about appreciating the moment we're in, even if difficult. I strongly believe that if we started each day with a mind focused on gratitude, meditating on all the things we appreciate, our outlook on the day ahead would be completely changed. As we begin to feel the cloud of dissatisfaction and unhappiness move its way over us, we have a choice and can shift the energy. We can choose sunlight and happiness by redirecting our focus to the positive; a simple, yet life-changing, choice.

Don't allow life's circumstances to deprive you of gratitude and happiness. There's always something to be thankful for. And like my friends in the Philippines, I try to find opportunities to *"Give thanks in all circumstances; for this is the will of God in Christ Jesus for you"* (1 Thessalonians 5:18).

Today, I resolve to be grateful despite my circumstances.

Entry | TWELVE

Dear Discontentment,

You apply unnecessary tension to my life and make me anxious about the future. You play a part in my failure to find satisfaction.

As I was walking one day, I watched ahead as this little girl, who appeared to be learning to walk, became more and more pleased with herself with each step she took. She beamed with excitement. Before she could look up at her mother to see an approving face smiling back, she noticed something colorful on the ground. She stopped and picked up a beautiful flower. She proceeded to smell it and, proud of her finding, she showed her parents her new treasure.

In that moment, I was reminded that at one point, each of us was as content with life as the little girl before me. But somewhere along the line, life stripped us of our ability to find pleasure in the simplest of things. The little girl was living in such a beautiful moment, appreciating the littlest of treasures most people would walk right past, or even step on. Right then I asked myself: *Am I walking so fast through life that I can't see the beauty in it? Am I so focused on all the things I want to change that I am not taking the time out each day to appreciate all the blessings? Are my expectations so high, I've disregarded the small victories along the way?*

It is so important that we find contentment in our daily lives, and we can do this by intentionally choosing to do so every day. I challenge you to choose contentment and practice it every day.

Socrates said, "He who is not contented with what he has, would not be contented with what he would like to have." I have learned to stop focusing on the aspects of my life that I want changed, and to honor the present and my current process. As this quote alludes to, I have realized that at times I have confused discontentment with ambition, convincing myself that my ambition was responsible for my tendency to yearn for more, to achieve more, and always eager to be more. In reality, this behavior was merely my inability to be content in my present.

Early in my marriage, I would express to my husband my aspirations for the future. When thinking of our future, I always felt behind in the goals we aimed to accomplish, goals like buying a house, starting a family, earning more income, and traveling more often. As I spoke with an undertone of haste to him about my concerns, his answer was always, "We will cross that bridge when we get there."

His words frustrated me. I didn't want to wait for the bridge. I wanted to run to it, cut corners, or jump trails to get to the bridge as fast as we possibly could. I would share with him stories of friends that were doing the things I thought we should already be doing. The comparisons always left me feeling like my achievements thus far were inadequate and as a result of that frustration, I placed an unfair amount of pressure on my husband. This chain-reaction of discontent caused some turmoil in my life and I became a prisoner to destructive thoughts.

It really wasn't until I had children that I understood contentment. For the first time in my life, I was excited for what the future would bring but I wasn't trying to hurry the moment. I wanted to pause time and soak in all the memories, because if there's one thing you learn while watching your kids grow up, it's that time has wings.

Additionally, as life began to unfold, I realized that had I received or accomplished all the things I had once wanted to happen so quickly, I wouldn't have been prepared and I most definitely would not have appreciated them. It was more evident to me that the success my family and I were now experiencing existed because we didn't rush the process, cut corners, and jump onto another trail.

Dear Discontentment

I now recognize the importance of accepting the present and I am thankful for a husband who helped me stay the course. I understand that everything I have experienced was by design; it was necessary for my growth. And as I grew more content, I found more joy in life, I was less anxious about things to come, and I had greater appreciation for the goals we accomplished.

Like that little girl learning to walk, I try to stop along the way and appreciate the areas blooming in my life. I aim to be more deliberate about living by Philippians 4:6-7, which reads: *"Do not be anxious about anything, but in every situation, by prayer and petition, with thanksgiving, present your requests to God. And the peace of God, which transcends all understanding, will guard your hearts and your minds in Christ Jesus."*

Today, I resolve to show contentment in all areas of my life and will release destructive expectations.

Entry | THIRTEEN

Dear Misunderstood,

You tell me that I need to constantly justify my actions and over-explain decisions I've made. You convince me to apologize for the way I am perceived and for things I may not have done, just to keep the peace.

I sat quietly, ear pressed to the phone, as I listened to my friend share that she was hurt by some of my recent actions. Mind you, prior to this conversation, I had no idea I had upset her. I was completely unaware that anything I had done (or not done, for that matter) had negatively impacted her in any way. However, from her point of view, I had hurt her deeply.

As I processed what she was saying, my initial reaction was to apologize for making her feel bad and for the potential adverse effect it may have had on our friendship. And so, I did apologize, and the conversation eventually ended.

The Rib

However, as the days passed, as I do with most
things I replayed and over-analyzed
the conversation in my head. It just wasn't
sitting right with me. I came to realize that
the shift my friend felt in me was due to
the shift I was experiencing in my life.

At that time in my life, I was not intentionally
making decisions to have an impact on anyone
other than myself, and all of the decisions
I made were necessary. In contemplating
the situation with my friend, I realized that
sometimes, growth and life's circumstances
might cause you to have to reroute
the trajectory of your life, and in doing so, you
may find that people who were once on
the same path as you no longer are. And
the totality of what they believe to be the cause
for your shift as a person, where they stand in
your life, and even where they are in theirs,
may impact how they respond to you. It may
lead to your being misunderstood.

I realized that I was being misunderstood.
Assumptions and misunderstandings about

the current direction of my life fed my friend's emotional response. A younger me would have stood by my apology, continued to have checked in, and worried nonstop about how my future decisions would impact the status of our friendship. Now, however, having gone through various life experiences that have helped me mature and understand that I cannot control another's perception of me, all I can do is stand in my truth.

I decided I would have one more conversation with my friend. I wanted to express to her that while I acknowledge her feelings and hope our friendship would be able to withstand the current shift in our lives, I would not apologize for who I was becoming. I planned to ask her to consider her assumptions and how they may be contributing to her perceptions of the situation.

This time, during our call she sat listening intently to me as I expressed my truths. She was quiet, and what usually would have felt like an uncomfortable stillness or lull in the conversation, actually felt more like validation. She was listening and digesting what I was saying.

As the conversation ended and I hung up the phone, I reminded myself that I could not control what happened from here; some people will choose to dig their heels in, assuming and misunderstanding no matter what is said or done. However, I felt better knowing that I wasn't apologizing unnecessarily just to keep the peace.

As a Christian, I believe God puts us in situations to strengthen us in areas where we need to grow. In the past, I have been one who shrinks herself to make others feel more comfortable, and often ended up feeling diminished by, and beneath, others. It took me some time to realize that God doesn't want the understanding of our worth to come from the acceptance or approval of others. Instead, He wants it to come from within, and—more importantly—from Him.

Now, in the moments when I feel misunderstood, it has helped me to hold onto the Bible verse, *"O Lord, you have searched me and known me. You know my sitting down and my rising up. You understand my thought afar off. You comprehend my path and my lying down, and are acquainted with all my ways"* (Psalms 139: 1-3). I then pray that my circle be filled with those that assume the best intent, are patient with me through my periods of growth, and encourage me to stand in my truth, as I support them to do the same.

Today, I resolve to stand tall in who I am and to never apologize for who I am becoming.

Entry | FOURTEEN

Dear Envy,

You are the source of constant comparison, and I am exhausted. As a result, I feel unaccomplished, not good enough, and as though I will never amount to anything.

I stood there, looking at my reflection in the full-length mirror, critiquing everything about myself. From my curves, or lack thereof, to my kinky hair, to the darker hues of my skin, I picked at everything I thought made me different from all the other 16-year-olds who would attend a pool party with me in just a few hours. And as I stared at my reflection, I could feel myself sinking deeper and deeper into the depths of self-consciousness and insecurity.

I debated going to the party. If I didn't go, I thought I'd be classified as an outcast because at that age I just knew that missing a big event like the pool party would set me apart from everyone else. What would be said about me?

The Rib

How would I explain to my friends why I didn't
show up? I didn't want to deal with
the repercussions, so I decided to go.

When I got to the party and saw the girls with
their perfect bodies, perfect hair, and perfect
skin, not to mention all the boys that seemed
to be captivated by them, I sank further into
my insecurities. I put on a fake smile and
explained that I wouldn't be swimming
because I didn't feel like doing my hair;
the quintessential and widely accepted black-
girl excuse. However, hearing myself say that
aloud made it clear that this was just another
way of distancing myself from the norm. After
the party, I went home and cried about not
fitting in, about every one of my differences
that I had, over time, convinced myself were
not acceptable. All I wished for was that
I simply just fit in.

This insecurity about who I was, a black girl in
a predominately white community, stayed
with me until adulthood. I admired and envied

so many others. I held their physical attributes and accomplishments above my own.

Inside, I felt as though I should apologize for who I was, so outwardly I began to do things to make sure I fit in. I would straighten my kinky hair. I would extreme-diet in hopes of becoming an acceptable size. I would stay in the shade in summer to avoid getting any darker.

As I grew deeper into who I was as a woman, my journey allowed me to be surrounded by women who did not apologize for who they were. They taught me to stand strong in who I was and to not only learn how to accept my differences, but to fully embrace and love them. I realized that my thinking as a youth had negatively affected me in so many ways, one of them being that I had become unable to admire another's successes without feeling like it took away from my own.

This was not the person I wanted to be. I did not want to be one who wanted others to have

less so that I could feel like I had more.
I realized I needed to learn confident
admiration, which to me is the ability to
respect another's journey without feeling as
though it somehow impedes your own. This
practice meant that I could admire another's
physical beauty, beauty completely different
from mine, and realize that just because
I didn't look the same did not mean I wasn't
beautiful.

Gaining this peace through confident
admiration helped me grow stronger in who
I am. I am now able to hold my head higher
and push further in my journey because I am
no longer creating constant pressure for
myself to fit into someone else's mold. I stand
stronger in who I am and my own unique path.
I hope to change the narrative that we,
especially women, have grown accustomed to:
that it is better to conform than to stand out.

As I think about how I want my daughter and
son to live their lives, I want them to
understand that it is perfectly okay to never fit

in and always stand out. And that standing out and living their truths loudly and boldly won't take away from their successes, character, or beauty, but will rather serve to enhance every aspect of their lives. It is also important to me that they understand that personal confidence and confident admiration of others can coexist, and will contribute to nurturing the ground they are rooted in, allowing them to fully bloom into the beautiful flowers they are meant to become.

Today, I resolve to turn envy into confident admiration.

Entry | FIFTEEN

Dear Over-committed,

You encourage me to believe that always filling my cup to the brim is acceptable and admired, and that my commitments somehow define my success and aptitude.

I came to my mother begging her to let me off the hook from some of my extracurricular activities. I was only eight years old but I understood that I was over-involved to the point that I was no longer enjoying anything I was part of. She honored my wishes and we cut back significantly. It was this moment of my life that I reflected on recently as I took part in a painting class with some friends.

As we stood before the blank canvases, it was hard to believe that by the end of the class they'd be colorful and vibrant works of art— especially the one from a non-artist such as me. Yet, as I looked at my empty canvas, I was

struck by the beauty of potential,
the possibility of what could be.

Our instructor told us to begin with
the background. We had free reign, but she
made sure to caution, "Remember, there is
beauty in simplicity." She was right. Staring at
the blank canvas, I wanted to fill all the white
space. However, with the instructor's advice in
mind, I slowly dipped my brush into a few
colors and with light strokes, I added them to
my canvas. I even left glimpses of white to
shine through.

While painting, I reflected on that time I felt
my life was too filled-in and I asked myself if
there were currently any areas in my life
where I could free up some space on my
canvas.

It is hard to not overextend ourselves when we
live in a society that encourages extreme
multitasking, over-participation, constant
career growth and business expansion, and
increased social circles. And while all of these

things are important, it is also important that we create the space in our lives to re-energize and to engage in self-care. By doing so, we restore our energy bank and give ourselves the time to check in, evaluate if our needs are being met, and truly put our best foot forward.

We must be careful not to over-commit and instead be deliberate and selective about what we participate in. I have learned to rid myself of FOMO (the fear of missing out) because I trust that whatever is meant for me will not pass me by. I have an appreciation for the blank canvases in my life and now I realize that sometimes the most beautiful art stems from the darkest and most challenging places. It speaks to the experiences of the artist and tells a story.

I also recognized that by leaving space on my canvas I allow God to participate in the masterpiece unfolding.

Today, I resolve to welcome the blank spaces on my personal canvas because they allow room for growth.

Entry | SIXTEEN

Dear Guilt,

You deny me the ability to enjoy the moment. Because of you, I constantly replay past missteps in my mind, leaving me feeling unworthy, unequipped, and inadequate.

As a new mother, I placed an incredible amount of pressure on myself. I never quite gave myself the credit I deserved and often criticized myself for my choices.

Guilt began to take root in my life like never before. I felt guilty for wanting to pursue my master's degree. I felt guilty for going back to work. I felt guilty for putting my child in day care. I felt guilty that I didn't have as much energy for my wifely responsibilities. I felt guilty for doing anything for myself.

I just felt guilt all day long. I was trying to be the best for everyone around me but I never felt adequate within. The guilt quickly turned to anxiety and depression and honestly, I just wanted to run away from it all. The guilt quickly grew, slowly blinding me to all the positives in my life until I could see only negatives.

After sensing a strong shift in my confidence and lull in my spirit, I realized something needed to change. I was becoming a prisoner of guilt. So, in order to regain my freedom, the first thing I knew I had to do was to admit guilt's presence in my life and identify the source. I was ready to dig deep and evaluate the cause of my guilt.

In some instances guilt occurs because of the decisions we make. Many times these are emotional decisions that feel like the best choice in the moment; however, later we realize it wasn't. In other instances, guilt arises from the constant pressures we place on ourselves. In my opinion, this is the most dangerous type of guilt because it infects our minds and contributes to negative self-talk, such as telling ourselves that we will never be good enough.

Dear Guilt

In my case, once I realized that I was completely overwhelmed and had placed too many unreasonable demands on myself, I was able to start freeing myself of some of the self-imposed guilt. I had to reprioritize and let some of those things go. And in doing so, one of my decisions was to hit PAUSE on my career. Although a very difficult decision, I knew it was necessary for my overall well-being.

For others, eliminating guilt may only come by seeking forgiveness or confronting past hurts. This may require counseling, having difficult conversations, or perhaps providing yourself isolation from any current distractions, in which you can find the space and time for deeper self-reflection.

It is important to trust yourself and be patient throughout the process because breaking down the effects of guilt is an internal process that will take time. Living life guilt-free allows us to feel the benefits of grace. The freedom of living a grace-centered life allows me to let go

of expectations of being perfect and extend
the same grace to others.

***Today, I resolve to forgive myself and to free
myself from guilt.***

Dear Resentment,

You fill me with feelings of negativity and intolerance. You hold me back from the freedom that is found in forgiveness and gratitude.

Late in the evening, I had put my daughter to sleep and called my husband, as we routinely did when he was traveling for work, to catch up on the day's events. I told him about all the new things our daughter was doing and how busy she seemed to keep me on a daily basis. I rushed through my words to ask him about his day and work because anything I was doing seemed so elementary in comparison to his responsibilities.

As he spoke, I could hear the enthusiasm in his voice about his profession and the things it allowed him to see and do. As he shared about his experiences in different cities, meeting new people, and staying in the nicest hotels, I could feel the jealousy welling up within.

The Rib

Not wanting him to sense my envy, I told him
I was tired and quickly ended the call. Lying in
bed that night and thinking about my feelings
during our call, I realized that I was allowing
my jealousy to turn into resentment.

I questioned every decision I had made about
my career path and my significance as The Rib.
Had I made a mistake? Did my husband
recognize the sacrifices I had made? Did he
realize that my sacrifices were helpful in his
ability to pursue his career while also
important to the function of our family?
I wondered if he ever wished he were in my
shoes, like I often wished I were in his.
The resentment overwhelmed me and I wept
until I fell asleep.

Truth be told, as I transitioned from my career
to being at home full-time, the resentment was
the biggest hurdle I had to overcome.
I expected many things, but resentment was
not one of them.

Dear Resentment

When I made the decision to leave nursing, I knew it was the best thing for our family and it was what I wanted to do; no one forced me. My husband fully supported me in whatever choice I was to make, whether that was to continue working or stay at home with our children.

So, why now was I resentful? Well, I realized it was because I was focusing on the things I had lost, rather than all that I had gained. To be stuck in a losing mentality made it impossible for me to see my wins and success, and it stole my optimism for the future.

I thought about times in my life when I had felt such a strong sense of resentment, and they were usually when I'd had my heart broken in relationships or in situations where I felt I deserved better but came out short. However, I realized that in order for me to freely move forward, I had to release the resentment. Knowing that I had done so in the past gave me confidence that I could do it again. I decided to

make this a focus in my daily prayers and
I asked God to help me release my resentment.

One day as I was praying through my
resentment, there was a clear whisper in my
ear, saying, "Count it all joy and choose to be
grateful." It was clear to me in that moment
that gratitude would be the remedy.

When I consciously switched my focus to
the things I was thankful for, I no longer felt
deficient in any area. Instead, I felt abundance
and acceptance. I recognized that I am grateful
for my past hurts because they taught me
a deeper meaning of love. I am grateful for my
husband's career, giving me the opportunity to
be a fully present parent at home with our
children and enjoy the priceless moments.

And though I am not currently practicing, I am
grateful for my career. It has taught me lessons
of empathy, compassion, and leadership, and
has allowed me to impact the lives of others.
My work as a nurse is something I will always

be proud of and something that can never be taken away from me.

I choose to no longer allow the weeds of resentment to take root in my garden. Instead, I choose to saturate my soil with gratitude. And since doing so, the weeds have begun to dissolve and my eyes are fully opened to the beautiful things that are blooming all around me.

Today, I resolve to cleanse myself of the past and walk into the future with a spirit of thankfulness.

Entry | EIGHTEEN

Dear Self,

My journey thus far has taught me that allowing myself to freely express my emotions has impelled my growth; it has allowed me to bloom. I refuse to live in fear, calling me to question my unique abilities and what it will mean to expose my truth. Now, I confidently acknowledge that God created me for a specific purpose, and everything I have experienced thus far has made me the person that I am. Even when I feel inadequate and question the path I am currently walking, I choose to trust in God's plan: that everything I am experiencing is preparing me and allowing me to fulfill my purpose.

I vow to continually allow myself to bend, mold, and bloom through the process, recognizing that I am a masterpiece in the making and that rushing the process only suppresses my full potential.

I am aware that my past has created a pathway to my purpose. I understand that at times to experience joy I've had to experience sadness, and through challenges I've gained newfound strength. I fully surrender to the journey, opening myself to new opportunities, while releasing anything that no longer serves me.

Today, I resolve to embrace my God-given gifts, and affirm that I was created for a purpose: I am The Rib.

CPSIA information can be obtained
at www.ICGtesting.com
Printed in the USA
BVHW091710151219
566719BV00009B/149/P